D1558373

SHAUNA

Written by **B. Keith Fulton**

Art by **Jerry Craft**

B.K. Fulton • Richmond

SHAUNA

Written by B. Keith Fulton
Illustrated by Jerry Craft

Text copyright ©2015 by B. Keith Fulton
Cover art and interior illustrations copyright ©2015 by Jerry Craft

Visit us on the web at
www.myshauna.com

Follow on Twitter @myshaunabook

Summary: This book is an adaptation of a poem written by the author when he was 16 years old. He was inspired by his sister Shauna, who was born with Rett syndrome. Unable to speak or walk on her own, the gift of Shauna's life and her family's love for her continues to encourage and bless many.

ISBN-13: 978-0-9862162-0-6
ISBN-10: 0986216208

Library of Congress Control Number: 2014919914

First Edition
Printed in the United States

DEDICATION

This book is dedicated to my youngest sister, Shauna, who without words, taught me to be a better man.

I believe that to whom much is given, much is expected (Luke: 12:48). When I was younger, I thought the "much" was a specific thing – for example, an ability to sing, dance, jump high, or play an instrument. As I matured, I realized that the "much" was actually life itself. If you woke up this morning, you have been given a great gift. You have the gift of *life*.

Whether you are old or young, male or female, fully able or have some disabilities, if you woke up, you are on the hook. No excuses. Your job is to live your life to the fullest. Our sons and daughters are depending on us to show them how they can accomplish each and every one of their dreams.

A gazing
little boy
stopped
and
asked:

Yes, adjusting her position in her wheelchair.

Yes,
adjusting
her
gaze
toward

HEAVEN.

In
your
new
found
wisdom ...
don't
count
me
out.

... because **I am**

LOVED!

B. KEITH FULTON

AUTHOR: B. Keith (BK) Fulton is a successful communications and entertainment executive. He has held senior leadership, technology and policy development positions in industry, government, and the non-profit sectors. In 2011, BK was named one of the "50 Most Influential African-Americans in Technology." His influential papers on technology are permanently archived at the Smithsonian Institute. BK holds a Bachelor's degree, a Master of Science degree, and a Juris Doctorate. He serves on the boards of Virginia Tech, Bon Secours Health Systems, the Virginia Chamber of Commerce and numerous other civic, social and business boards. He is the father of twin boys, Joshua and Terrell, and married to Jacquelyn E. Stone. They live in Richmond, VA.

His sister Shauna currently lives at home with their parents, Bennie and Flora Fulton, in Hampton, VA.

For more information please visit www.myshauna.com

JERRY CRAFT

ARTIST: Jerry Craft has illustrated and / or written more than two dozen children's books, comic books and board games. Most recent is a middle grade novel co-written with his two teenage sons, Jaylen and Aren called: "The Offenders: Saving the World While Serving Detention!" — an adventure story that teaches kids about the effects of bullying. He is the creator of Mama's Boyz, a comic strip that won four African American Literary Awards and was distributed by King Features from 1995 - 2013. He also illustrated "The Zero Degree Zombie Zone" for Scholastic.

For more information email him at jerrycraft@aol.com or visit www.jerrycraft.net

CPSIA information can be obtained at www.ICGtesting.com
Printed in the USA
LVOW05*0833081015

457415LV00020B/72/P